GUIDES

WOODFRAME FURNITURE RESTORATION

Alan Smith

EBUR
PRES

For Christine

First published by Ebury Press
National Magazine Company Limited
National Magazine House
72 Broadwick Street
London W1V 2BP

All statements in this book giving information and advice are
believed to be true and accurate at the time of going to press, but
neither the authors nor the publishers can accept legal responsibility
for errors or omissions.

Conceived and produced by
Swallow Publishing Limited
32 Hermes Street, London N1

Editor: Anne Yelland
Editorial consultant: Tom Seavey
Art director: Glynis Edwards
Designer: Barry Walsh
Illustrators: Hussein Hussein, Aziz Khan, Coral Mula, Rob Shone
Photography: Jon Bouchier
Studio: Barry Walsh
Picture research: Liz Eddison

ISBN 0 85223 414 7

Typeset in Palatino by Dorchester Typesetting Group Ltd
Origination RCS Graphics Ltd
Printed and bound in Italy by New Interlitho, Milan

Contents

The idea of restoration

Restoration means different things to different people. To the antique dealer, for example, it often means work done to improve the saleability of items, whereas to the museum curator it means re-creating the original appearance of a piece, regardless of whether it is fit for use. The ordinary furniture craftsman, working for his own pleasure, should try to tread the middle path, attempting to preserve the beauty and usefulness of his possessions, but avoiding alterations which conflict with the original use and appearance of the piece. Whenever a restorer replaces missing parts, he should always ask himself if they are like the originals. The same is true of the finish applied to a piece. Polyurethane varnish, for instance, is a modern material, and has no place in restoration work. The restorer who uses traditional tools and techniques, with an understanding of the methods of the old craftsman, can rest assured that his work will gradually blend with the original piece.

In order to make replacement parts, it will help if you can acquire a stock of old furniture scraps; old wood, and antique hinges and handles, will all blend into their surroundings more readily than newer items. These pieces need not be expensive – in fact, they can often be taken away free from salerooms or gleaned from skips (trash containers). Do not overlook the usefulness of old tools either, as restoration work often involves cutting into wood that may conceal nails or other metal parts.

Skill alone will not make a good restorer. In order to improve his work the restorer should learn something about the history of furniture and furniture-making. This will help when making decisions about the correct form of replacement parts, and in creating an authentic period finish. Finally, remember that the most valuable tools in the restorer's kit are the eyes. 'Eyes first, hands last' is a good general rule, and an hour or two spent looking really closely at a piece of furniture can help immensely when it comes to deciding what is to be done. Keep a record of what you do in a notebook; over a few projects this will build up into a file of useful information for future reference. In this way, you can profit from your mistakes, and not repeat them.

Left: *Careful repair and painstaking finishing have transformed this pine chiffonier from derelict to delight. Major jobs like this take time, but are very satisfying.*

What can be restored?

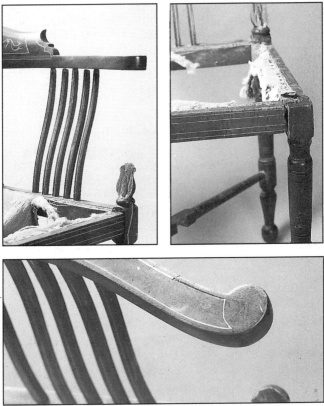

This delicate corner chair shows many repairable faults. Open joints (top right) round the seat frame may only need cleaning and regluing, and missing turnings (top left) are soon made on a lathe. Repairing faults like the missing inlay takes care and patience.

In theory, there are no limits to the art of the restorer. In practice, however, the craftsman is bound by limits of time and skill to simpler tasks. Any piece of furniture which is more or less complete is suitable for restoration and we list here the types of repair which are covered in greater detail in the rest of the book.

Broken legs especially of the turned type are often fairly easy to replace. Some chairs have very elaborately shaped rear legs, which carry on to form part of the chair back, but even these can be made anew or repaired if you are patient and careful.

Missing frame parts are quite common on chairs and tables, especially the dainty small tables popular in the nineteenth century. Straight parts are easy to replace, but it is difficult to arrive at the correct shape for some parts. Included in the text are tips to help you do this.

Broken or damaged doors come in all shapes and sizes. There are far too many different door types to cover them all in a single book, but the most common types are detailed. Usually, however, the problem is one of loose hinges and cracked panels, and full descriptions of how to repair these faults are given.

Loose joints, often the result of shrinkage or glue failure, are built-in features of most old furniture. The usual symptom is a noticeable resilience. This is not important if the piece is for ornament only, but if it is to be used every day, careful dismantling and regluing are called for.

Cracked panels are almost always found in old furniture which has been exposed to modern central heating or air-conditioning. Good panel repairs may involve major dismantling of other sound parts, and need to be approached with care. Nevertheless, methods of making near invisible repairs are given.

Missing veneers are a common problem. Metal inlays, and patterned or plain veneers of thin wood, are very prone to damage, and may become loose, or even lost. The job of replacing them is painstaking, but basically not difficult once the techniques involved are revealed.

Dented and stained surfaces are found on almost every piece of old furniture, and some of the methods of dealing with them properly belong in a book on furniture refinishing. Basic problems and solutions are discussed, however, as are first steps in repolishing damaged wood, and matching new parts to old.

Do not let lack of experience in restoring put you off attempting even difficult repairs. Because they are relatively free from the pressures of finance and time that dog the professional, much of the finest work in this field is done by home workers. Following the step-by-step techniques given here will enable anyone with basic woodworking skills to make a start in this, the most wide-ranging and fascinating of all the wood trades.

The tools of the trade

Most restoration work can be done in the home without an extensive toolkit or elaborate facilities, but warm surroundings and good light are important. If you lack space, a folding bench and vice (vise) will do. Tools, whether old or new, are expensive, but treated well they will last almost indefinitely.

Regular woodworking tools – most of which you will probably already have – are the basis of the restorer's kit: a panel and a fine tenon saw; a coping saw and a small hacksaw; a hand or electric drill with variable speed; a carpenter's brace; two screwdrivers, one of the long slim electrician's type and one middle-sized; a jack plane; a small block plane; a shoulder plane; a set of bevel-edge chisels; a cross peen hammer; and a wooden mallet comprise the basic toolkit.

The problems of the restorer are often different from those of the cabinet-maker, and to tackle restoration effectively, you will need some special tools. Many of these can be made simply at home.

Spring clamps can be cut from old upholstery springs with a small hacksaw. Cut various sizes from a full circle to just over half a circle. They can be used in various ways as clamping aids.

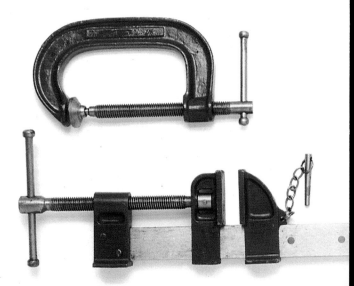

Rubber webbing is a powerful way of holding awkward items while you are gluing them. Thin strips can be cut from old auto inner-tubes by slicing round in a spiral pattern with a sharp knife. Rings cut to make large bands will also be useful. Alternatively, buy some large rubber bands. Webbing is wound over the parts to be joined and pulled tighter with each turn. A few turns will exert a powerful pressure without leaving scars on the surface.

Folding wedges are a lightweight alternative to sash cramps. Simple to make, they are used for all kinds of bigger cramping jobs, like rejointing table tops. In use, the bottom rail is set to a handy length and the wedges are tapped in to increase the pressure.

The scratch-stock is used to make mouldings, or for cutting small grooves. The two handles are made to a comfortable shape, and cutters are filed as required from scrap steel.

A veneer hammer is used when you are re-laying larger pieces of veneer. Its size and shape are not critical, but make the blade from a smooth-surfaced strip of brass.

Sash and g-cramps (clamps) are very useful. If you plan to buy some, get the lighter types, since many joiner's cramps are too heavy for delicate items.

A gluepot, for hot animal (scotch) glue, can be improvised from an ovenware jar, and an old pan. A good small brush will be needed for applying glue. Animal glue is the best for restoration work, and well worth the trouble of preparing it. Details of how to mix animal glue are given on p. 22.

Miscellaneous tools, most of which are in the handyman's toolkit already, will also be needed on occasions. Files, pincers, and electrician's pliers and cutters are useful. A sturdy old screwdriver will help lift tacks, and a few old chisels will protect fine tools from damage where you suspect old nails might be hidden.

Clamps like these are expensive but vital aids to repair and reassembly. Cheaper wooden cramps are sometimes available.

Materials

Glues and fillers

Animal (scotch) glue is the professional restorer's first choice for all wood to wood joints, and is also used for hand veneering, and bone and shell inlay.

PVA (yellow) glue is a good second-best to animal glue. If you use this, remove all traces of old animal glue, since the two do not mix well.

Resin glues can be used where strength is at a premium (for example, on chair back repairs).

Two-part epoxy glues stick almost anything, but may make problems for future restorers, since they are difficult to remove.

Cyanoacrylates are suitable for small repairs to inlay and moulding, *not* for structural work.

Starch paste, *not* the modern 'cellulose' type, is good for laying baize, leather, and paper linings.

'Clam' is a modern paperhanging paste. It is expensive but a strong substitute for starch.

Contact (impact) glues can be useful for lining work but are not 'sympathetic' materials for restoration.

Beaumontage or hard stopping is a mix of beeswax, resin and shellac. See pp. 24-5 for details on use.

Clay-based fillers, a mix of clay, glue and water, are good for *small* splits or dents.

Cellulose wax is a modern synthetic wax material suitable for use under all kinds of finishing material.

Beeswax, the traditional filler for all small blemishes, is not suitable for use under varnish or cellulose, unless it is sealed with french polish (shellac).

Polishes and waxes

Beeswax polish is a mix of beeswax and Mexican turpentine, and may be modified with other waxes. Use it with a duster for routine cleaning (not more than four times a year) or with steel wool for refinishing.

Silicone wax polish should be avoided for old furniture. Under certain conditions of temperature and humidity, it can deteriorate. This 'bloom' is best treated with a reviving solution (see pp. 74-5).

French polish or shellac solution is a mixture of shellac resin and methylated spirit (wood alcohol) and is available in many grades.

Shellac or 'spirit' varnishes are a variety of french polish mixed so as to be suitable for application with a brush. They can give good results if *carefully* used.

Copal varnish is the traditional material for finishing some American furniture.

Polyurethane varnish is modern and tough and should only be used where pieces are given hard daily use.

Cleaning materials

Steel wool can be used with wax for polishing wood, or with a little olive oil on corroded metal parts. Use only the very finest (0000) grade.

Pumice powder is mildly abrasive and can be used to remove paint stains and so on from polished surfaces, and also for dulling glossy french polish.

Jeweller's rouge is mixed to a paste with olive oil, and used for polishing fine metals of all kinds.

Real soap flakes and warm water are the best and most gentle cleaning medium for all types of surface. Rinse off all traces of soap after use.

Best quality furniture wax, fine, soft steel wool, and old cotton cloth give the best results when polishing.

Techniques

Basic damage repairs

Restoration often involves dismantling, and the art of success here is to be methodical. Beware of nails, which were put into joints in the past. This problem is common, and trying to open a joint with a nail in can do a lot of damage. If a part feels rigid, glue is probably holding it firm. The safest way to open a good glued joint is to render the glue useless by washing it out, or melting it. Both modern PVA (yellow) glue, and animal (scotch) glue, soften when hot. Use boiling water, or after wetting the surface well, a gas torch. Be patient as wood is a poor conductor. If you have a workbench with a tail vice (vise), use the vice to prise (pry) apart chair and door frames. Fit the vice dogs inside the frame, and wind the jaws apart. The steady pull will open stubborn joints.

Another common problem which many people find difficult to deal with is opening up secret wedged tenon joints. Wedging may be used by restorers as a method of improving loose joints. The tenon is slotted and one or more small wedges put in. When the joint is reassembled, the wedges hit the base of the mortise, and are forced into the tenon, spreading it apart. This makes it difficult to take the joint apart again. The best method is to open the joint as far as possible, and cut the tenon. The cut should go into one of the slots, and you should be able to pull out the reduced width tenon, leaving the wedge and part of the tenon inside the mortise. The tenon can be glued back normally when you are reassembling.

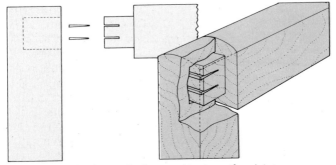

The secret wedged tenon is often used to strengthen joints.

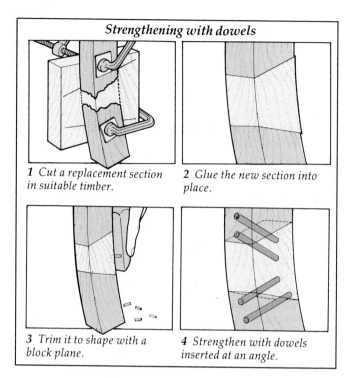

Strengthening with dowels

1 Cut a replacement section in suitable timber.

2 Glue the new section into place.

3 Trim it to shape with a block plane.

4 Strengthen with dowels inserted at an angle.

Strengthening methods

Large cracks give restorers difficult problems. Filling large splits with stopping will not be successful; the job may last a while, but the filling will eventually fall out, because the sides of the crack move independently. Lock the edges together with a dowel, then fill the split and repolish the surface.

Where panels are too thin to dowel, apply two layers of veneer to the back of the panel. The grain of each layer should run at right angles to its neighbour, and the three-ply sandwich you create should reduce the tendency of the panel to warp. Trim the veneer, then fill and polish the part.

Splits in cabinet ends and tops can sometimes be squeezed shut with a couple of strong clamps. The secret is to apply a very slight pressure over a long period. In these circumstances the glued joints in the piece gradually creep, and the split closes. Tighten the clamps twice a day, but don't hurry this part. When the split has closed, slacken off the clamps, glue the cleaned crack, and reclamp until the glue has set.

Replacing cloth and leather

Desks and tables covered with leather, or a type of fine felt cloth called baize, became fashionable in the eighteenth century. This type of surface was quieter and kinder than wood, and more suitable for fine glasses, card playing, or writing. At first linings were made from fairly heavy hides, but morocco leathers, glazed and beautifully coloured, soon became popular.

Removing the old cover is fairly straightforward. Lift up a corner, and simply tear it off. This will leave a residue of glue and fibres beneath that can be washed off with hot water. Allow the water to soak into the old paste for a few moments and then wipe it off.

Like veneer (see pp. 56-9), leather should be laid on a sound base, so this is the time to attend to holes or loose knots. Since repairs on defects here are unlikely to be seen, you can use a strong durable filler like autobody repair paste. This has the advantage that it is easy to rub down flat – the slightest bump will be seen through the new cover.

The old method of fixing leather tops, with starch paste, has yet to be bettered. Modern contact glues can be used, but an inadvertent crease put into the surface as you lay it is impossible to remove, and any splash of adhesive on to a polished part of the work will destroy

This Victorian desk has a plain leather top without a border, the simplest kind to lay and trim.

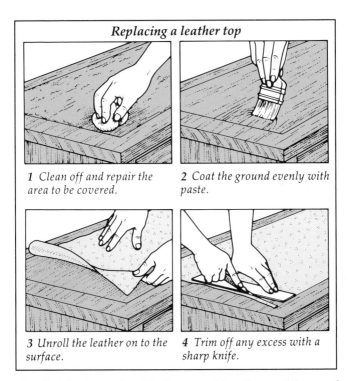

Replacing a leather top

1 Clean off and repair the area to be covered.

2 Coat the ground evenly with paste.

3 Unroll the leather on to the surface.

4 Trim off any excess with a sharp knife.

the finish. You should also consider the problems of following generations of restorers, who will find contact glue hard to shift.

You can make your own paste by adding enough tepid water to a cup of flour to make a thick, smooth sauce. Add about 500ml (1 pint) of boiling water, stirring as you go. The result should be translucent lump-free paste. Leather skivers (tops) are best ordered from a specialist supplier, who will add a tooled border if you wish.

Coat the ground evenly with paste – two thin coats are best – then lay the leather by unrolling it on to the surface. (Cloth is laid in the same way.) Take care to keep the roll straight, though the paste will allow for some adjustment. Use an iron, cool enough to bear on the palm of the hand, to press it down. Where the covering fits into a groove, you can push it firmly down with the rounded end of a steel rule. Trim off any surplus with a razor-sharp craft knife.

Finally, when you are laying cloth, keep the paste to a minimum because any excess will penetrate through and spoil the surface.

Project 1: Windsor chair

Solid wooden chairs

Country-made chairs with turned legs and backs, and shaped solid wooden seats, are found all over the world. One type of country chair, produced and sold in Britain in various styles for over three hundred years, is the Windsor chair. These chairs were also exported to the USA, where they influenced the development of American Windsor chairs. These, in turn, were the inspiration for the very similar Boston rocking chair. The seat was generally made from a single piece of elm, and the other parts from beech, ash, or occasionally, yew. All the jointed parts of the chair were turned on a crude foot-operated pole lathe and legs, arms, and back-sticks were fitted into holes bored with an auger.

Diagnosing faults

With simple items, many of the faults are immediately obvious, but nevertheless, the restorer should look carefully at every part of the piece for signs of damage, old repairs, and to ensure that the item is authentic. Search for nails or screws in the joints, worm damage, and loose parts. These must all be attended to, since a chair is more highly stressed than other pieces of furniture, and must be sound if it is to be used regularly. One or other of the turned parts may be missing, or may perhaps have been replaced with a similar, but not identical, part. New parts can be turned on a simple power-drill lathe attachment.

The chair illustrated had a broken leg, and almost all the joints were loose and creaking. The only way to fix failed chair joints properly is to take the chair apart, but we should emphasize here that complete dismantling is only called for when most of the chair joints have failed. Single joints can often be repaired without major surgery, by injecting fresh glue, or in the case of wedged joints, by cutting out the loose wedge and gluing and knocking a larger one into the slot.

Sometimes, the whole back frame will still be sound, in which case it may be possible to leave this in one piece and dismantle only the seat board and front legs. Windsor chairs, however, have no back frame, and the rear legs and the chair back are completely separate.

Left: *Produced in a variety of styles for over three hundred years, the Windsor chair is valued for its simple elegance and sturdy construction.*

Dismantling techniques

Dismantling old chairs is a nerve-racking job until you have had some practice. Clear a space to work in before you begin – it will help if you have a workbench big enough to lay the chair on. The best technique for the home restorer is to use a wooden mallet to drive the joints apart. The surface of the chair must be protected from bruising, so keep an old blanket or rug between the chair and bench and fix a scrap of carpet to the mallet with masking tape to soften the blows. If you take care to strike firmly and in the correct direction to open the joint, few joints will resist for long.

Removing chair legs

It is usually simplest when you are dismantling a chair to remove the legs first, since this gives better access to the underneath of the seat, where the more difficult arm-rest supports may be wedged in position. Lay the chair on its back, grasp one of the legs firmly in one hand and strike the underside of the seat smartly with the mallet. After a couple of blows, the leg ought to come out of its socket. It can then be separated from the

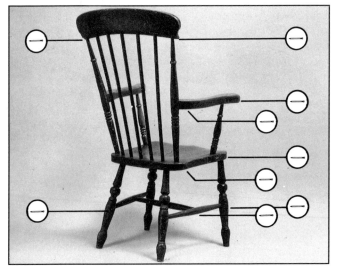

Any joint which fails to come apart after a couple of firm mallet blows is probably held together with a nail or dowel driven sideways through the joint. The photograph shows the most likely places to find nails in a chair.

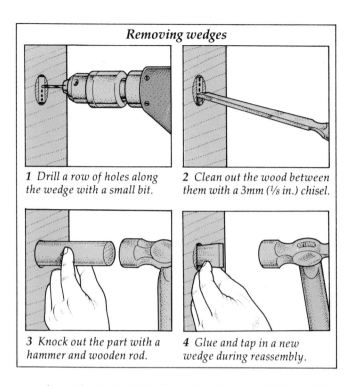

Removing wedges

1 Drill a row of holes along the wedge with a small bit.

2 Clean out the wood between them with a 3mm (1/8 in.) chisel.

3 Knock out the part with a hammer and wooden rod.

4 Glue and tap in a new wedge during reassembly.

stretchers that join it to the other legs, and laid aside. Work round the chair, removing each leg in turn.

It is a good idea, particularly when you first start, to put paper tape labels on each part so that you know where they come from. If any joint fails to come apart, examine it carefully, since this is a sign that it may be fastened together with a nail. This must be removed before the joint will part. Use a pair of sharp-nosed electrical cutters to get a grip on the nail; it may help to tap them into the surrounding wood with a hammer.

Removing the back and arms

The back and arms usually protrude through holes drilled right through the seat. When the chairs are made, the timber is slit with a saw up to the point where it enters the hole, and a small wedge knocked into the slit from beneath the seat. This wedge opens the slit out, effectively locking the parts together, and makes a very firm joint, which remains strong even after the glue has perished. The wedges, however, must be removed before the parts can be separated.

Cleaning the joints

Clean joint faces will contribute a great deal to a successful repair. If your chair has never been mended before, the glue in the joints will be the original animal (scotch) glue, which can easily be removed with hot water and a coarse cloth. Animal glue can be recognized by its brown toffee-like appearance and highly soluble nature. Chairs that have modern repairs may have been glued with PVA (yellow) resin, which can be identified by its semi-transparent, white colour and cheesy feel. You can use hot water or methylated spirits (wood alcohol) to remove PVA, but remember that spirit will also dissolve french polish from surfaces which show. The worst kind of glues to find in a repaired chair are the resin adhesives. These set like cement, by chemical reaction, are glass-hard and proof against all solvents. The only way in which they can be removed is by scraping or filing the glue from the joint surfaces.

Making a new leg

Windsor chairs have turned legs, and to make a new one you will need a lathe although for simple work the type sold as a power-drill attachment is adequate. You will also need a piece of beech, a little longer, thicker and wider than the biggest dimension of the original leg. Take the measurements of the surviving leg, or if both are missing, find a similar chair and copy the legs from that – about 500 × 50 × 50mm (20 × 2 × 2 in.) will usually be about right. Turn the wood to a smooth cylinder, by pressing the tool against the wood so that it brings off a steady stream of shavings.

Measure the main features from your pattern piece, and make bold lines with the lathe running. The small round features (called beads) are made with a skew-chisel. Always work so that the tool cuts from the larger diameter to the smaller. Working 'downhill' like this will result in a smoother surface. The larger vase-shaped details can be cut with the gouge, once again working downhill. Deep grooves at the top and bottom of the leg can be cut with a small gouge. When the work is finished, you can remove the waste at these points with a saw. Sand the work in the running lathe, using a long strip of sandpaper held firmly, and finish by burnishing it with a small stick of wood, pressed firmly against the spinning leg.

Turning a new leg

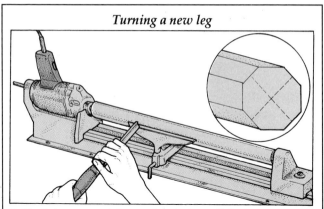

1 Mark the centre of the wood and plane off the corners. Then, using a gouge, turn the wood to a smooth cylinder.

2 Mark the details on the leg with a skew-chisel.

3 Check the size at several points with plywood gauges.

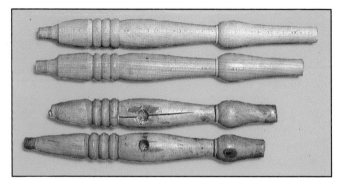

Turned with care, a new leg will match the size and shape of the old one perfectly.

Preparing glue

When the repairs are complete, the chair can be put together again. Animal glue is the most suitable adhesive for restoration work, but it will need to be prepared. Glue of this kind is always best when first made, so only make up a little at a time; for the average chair about 110g (4oz.) should be plenty. If you have bought cake glue, break up the lumps by putting them into a strong plastic bag and hammering it. (This will prevent the fragments flying in all directions.) Put the glue beads or broken lumps into a small container – a jam jar is the right size – and just cover them with cold water. Ideally, you should then leave the mixture to soak overnight. Stand the glue mixture in its container in a small saucepan half-full of cold water. Heat the pan gently, until the water is too hot to touch, but not boiling, and keep the water at this temperature. A small hotplate containing a spirit heater (alcohol lamp) or candle is ideal for this. When the glue has turned to an even brown soup, about the consistency of single (thin) cream, it is ready to use. You can buy special glue brushes, but if you do not have one, you can use a stiff bristle paintbrush to spread it with.

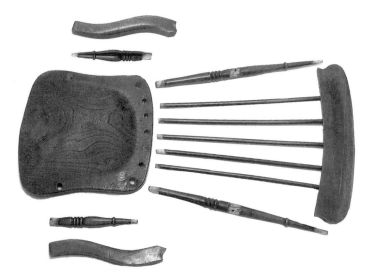

Speed is essential if you are using animal glue, so lay out all the pieces in order before you begin reassembling the chair.

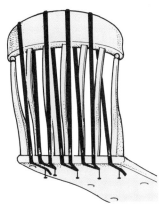

It is difficult to use sash-cramps on a chair back unless you make a saddle to hold them, so use rubber webbing to hold the pieces together while the glue dries. Knock some panel pins into the underside of the seat and wrap the webbing around them.

Reassembling the chair

It is difficult to make firm rules about reassembling chairs, since the details of their construction vary so much. Most chairs with arms are best put together from the top down, so if you dismantled the back, begin by regluing the back-slats and centre splat into the crest rail. Animal glue only works well when it is hot, so work quickly. Warming the parts briefly in the blast from a fan heater will give you more time to fit them together. When all the back is assembled, glue it into the seat-board. Lay this flat on the bench, and put a generous brushful of glue into the sockets. Take the back assembly and push the uprights into the seat. If you have difficulty with some of the slats, wrap a wad of carpet over the crest rail, and tap the back home with mallet blows. Still working as quickly as possible, insert the arm supports, without gluing them into the seat, and fit the unglued arm-rests into position – this will help to ensure the back is in the correct position.

The back will need clamping up tight, to ensure that all the parts are fully home. When you have clamped the back together, lay it on the bench and glue new hardwood wedges into the slots in the bottom of the main uprights. Examine the chair carefully to make sure everything is straight and set it aside for 24 hours.

The legs are fitted in much the same way as the back. Glue the stretchers in place first, and then insert pairs of freshly glued legs into the seat. Pull the whole assembly hard together with rubber straps. This final clamping should be done with the chair standing on a level floor to ensure that it does not dry out with a built-in twist.

Final touches

'Beauty is skin deep' is an expression the restorer should remember. Most of our judgements about the quality or looks of a piece of furniture are based on its surface appearance. For this reason, restorers always consider carefully the finish they give to their work. Indiscriminate stripping of the surface is not recommended, unless it has deteriorated due to damp or neglect, or in cases where a piece has been refinished with paint or varnish that is definitely not original. This may require research. Eighteenth-century Windsor chairs found in Britain, for example, were originally waxed or spirit varnished, while contemporary exports, for assembly in the USA, were usually painted black or green with line decoration.

Minor surface repairs

Whichever method of finishing you choose, surface damage will have to be made good. The ways of doing this are much the same, whether you are going to polish or paint the piece. The traditional filling material used for small holes – old nail or screw holes, for example – is hard stopping, or beaumontage, which is made from equal parts of beeswax and resin, and available from finishing specialists in a wide variety of colours. Make sure that the hole to be filled is free from dirt and grease before you start.

Small dents on exposed surfaces can often be repaired by wetting the surface of the dent and pressing the tip of a hot iron against it. The steam produced swells the wood fibres, and the dent may almost disappear. Larger cracks and holes should be repaired with an insert of wood, as described on pp. 41-2. Splits at the edge of a seat or table top will need reinforcing; the easiest way to do this is to bore a hole in the edge of the split part, and glue a dowel into it to unite the two parts as described on p. 13. This stops the crack from spreading and helps keep the filler in place.

Wax polishing

All furniture needs a finish of some sort and wax polishing is a simple technique appropriate for country-style furniture. Wash the piece down with a mixture of equal parts of turpentine and methylated

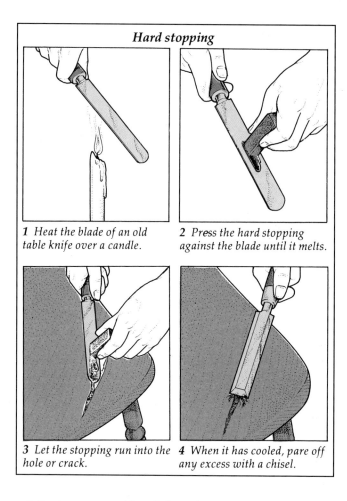

Hard stopping

1 Heat the blade of an old table knife over a candle.

2 Press the hard stopping against the blade until it melts.

3 Let the stopping run into the hole or crack.

4 When it has cooled, pare off any excess with a chisel.

spirits, to remove old polish and grease. Any remaining polished parts have probably been finished with oil varnish, which can only be removed with paint stripper. When the surface is clean and dry, sand it smooth with 240 grit paper. It is now ready for wax polishing. You can buy special wax from finishing suppliers, or you can make your own, as described on p. 75. The wax is best applied with a clean soft shoebrush. When the whole piece has been coated, rub it hard with a small pad of finest grade (0000) steel wool. A final burnish with a soft cloth will finish the job.

Waxing can be repeated as often as you like, but you should take care to avoid a build-up of sticky wax on the surface.

Project 2: Scrub-top table

The farmhouse table

The country-made table, with square or turned legs, has a history almost as long as that of the Windsor chair. British examples were generally made from pine, or more rarely, oak, while maple, or a mix of other local woods, were more common in America. The tops were usually made from a light wood. Such tables were used for the preparation of food, and proud cooks would scrub the top with hot water and lye soap until it was snowy-white. The legs were often painted, or stained and polished to a dark gloss.

Genuine old tables of this kind are still plentiful, and relatively inexpensive. However, strong interest in country furniture, and the simple structure of this kind of table, has led to many imitations. Regularly spaced nail marks are a sign that a top may have been made from old floorboards. Another guide is the thickness of the wood used to make the underframe; view wood thinner than 25mm (1in.) with suspicion.

Diagnosing faults

As these tables are of fairly standard construction, the same faults are common to them all. First, many have been painted at some time, and a good part of this may remain. If this is the case, paint stripping is the first task. Usually, the table top will be made up of at least four boards, and these will probably have shrunk apart, leaving gaps that may have been filled with plaster or putty. The best method of repair is to remove and refit the whole top. As the boards are often merely nailed to the frame this is not too difficult and, if the legs are loose or broken, the top will probably need to be removed in any case. Because this type of table was made for heavy use, the underframe is usually fairly sturdy, but the legs will probably have suffered damage, caused by the table being dragged around on floor-wash day. Frayed feet, and a worn look around the base of the legs, are usual. Finally, the drawer bottom, or the drawer supports, called runners, may be badly worn or missing. This job can be safely left until last.

Left: *Two variations of the farmhouse table, valued for its sturdy simplicity. The plain styling (top) is typical of American Shaker furniture. A drawer to hold the cook's tools (bottom) is common — and likely to be one of the restorer's major problem areas.*

Paint stripping

Stripping off old paint and polish is sometimes necessary, but should be done only when you are sure the surface is not original.

There are many different paint strippers on the market for home use, and most are suitable for restoration work; the important thing is to select the right one for the job at hand. Broadly speaking, there are two main types of liquid stripper – those which are washed off after use with water and those which are removed with white spirit (paint thinner). Both are suitable for solid timber furniture, but the spirit-washable kind is best for delicate articles, and wood-veneered or inlaid surfaces since water will soften the animal (scotch) glue used to lay the decoration. Commercial paint-stripping firms have proliferated in recent years. They usually strip paint by dipping the item in a large tank of hot caustic soda solution (lye water). While very effective, this is far too drastic for all but the sturdiest items. It is also unlikely that your furniture will get the same care as you would give it.

A stiff nylon-bristle brush can be used to remove water-soluble paint stripper.

Stripping techniques

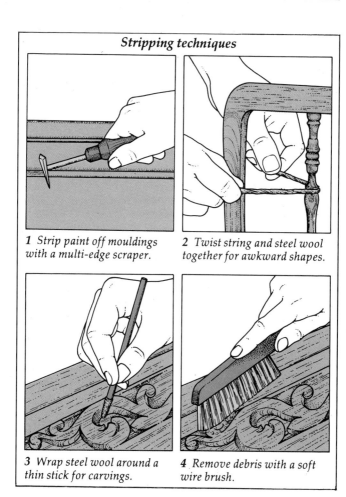

1 Strip paint off mouldings with a multi-edge scraper.

2 Twist string and steel wool together for awkward shapes.

3 Wrap steel wool around a thin stick for carvings.

4 Remove debris with a soft wire brush.

The best place to strip paint is outdoors, preferably in cool weather to prevent the stripper drying out too quickly. If space or the weather are against you, work in a well-ventilated room, without any form of heating, keep the window open and do not smoke. Cover the floor with plenty of old newspapers, and wear old clothes, gloves, and goggles. Follow the manufacturer's instructions carefully, and pay special attention to cleaning out all the awkward grooves and corners. Two or more applications of stripper may be needed for stubborn or thick paint, so ensure that you have plenty of materials, and cotton rags at hand. When you have finished, remove all traces of stripper from the piece – any residue will affect the quality of new polish.

Repairing the top

Unlike polished furniture, which would have been protected from harm, the scrub-top table was made to stand hard use. Hot water, grease, meat juices and kitchen tools will all have left their mark on the surface. One of the commonest results of this wear is that large gaps appear between the boards. The top may be held on by screws, or buttons, but the usual thing with country tables is for the top to be fixed down with old-style flat nails, called cut nails.

To remove a nailed top, tap a wide wood chisel into the small gap between the underside of the top, and the frame members. When the chisel has gone in about 25mm (1in.), pull steadily downwards on the handle, to separate top and frame. You can buy a special tool for separating boards, called a flooring bolster (pry-bar), if you would rather not try this with your favourite wood chisel. By working around the frame, prising (prying) the boards up inch-by-inch, you should be able to remove the whole top without damaging it. The old cut nails usually pull through the back of the top boards and remain in the framework of the table. They can easily be removed with pincers.

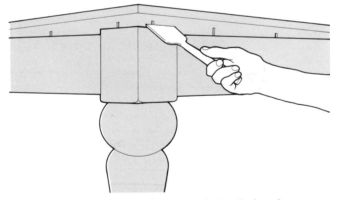

Work a flooring bolster into the joint and prise the board up.

Although some table tops are joined with tongue-and-groove joints, or more rarely, wooden dowel pins, the boards will usually come apart quite easily. Pour boiling water over stubborn joints before you prise them apart. Work from the back to avoid bruising the table face.

Improving the fit

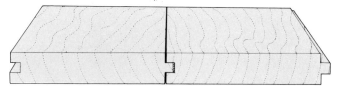

If the boards have shrunk apart, but the tongue is a tight fit, plane the tongue down to improve the appearance.

Where the tight spot is underneath the boards, cut away the surplus with a shoulder plane.

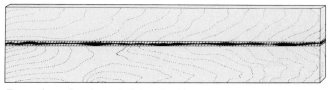

Dress along the edges of plain-edged boards with a sharp plane, set to take off fine shavings.

If the table-top boards are fastened together with pegs or tongue-and-groove joints, improving the fit of the parts is a fairly skilled task. With a tongue-and-groove jointed top, you must carefully clean out the groove, which may have filled with dust and food crumbs over the years. Test-fit the boards back together in the correct order, and pull them tightly together with at least three clamps. If the boards will still not close up, you will have to plane away the lower edge of the groove. Plain-edged boards without joints should be dressed along the edges with a sharp plane. Remove only a little wood at a time and test the fit of the boards as you work. Undercutting the edges slightly will improve the surface fit.

If your table has a dowel-jointed top, treat it in the same way; the only difference is that you will have to remove the dowels and replace them after you have dressed the edges. If the table needs no other attention, nail the top back in position, using old nails if possible.

Fixing the frame

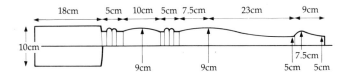

A measured sketch for a replacement leg. 'Hairline precision' is not vital; the eye will accept slight differences in legs more than 60cm (2ft) apart.

One or more of the legs of your table may be missing, or damaged beyond repair. Whole legs can be turned on a small lathe, as described on pp. 20-1, but for an item of this size it is better to make a measured sketch of the leg, and find a woodturner with a bigger machine. The Yellow Pages or local craft associations are good places to look. If the glue has simply failed, but the joint parts are still intact, all you need to do is clean up the joint faces with hot water, coat them with hot animal glue (see pp. 22-3) and reassemble. A convenient way of supporting the table is to lay it on its back, on top of a pair of trestles (saw horses), or across the workbench. The leg must be straight after gluing, so sight carefully along the frame and pull the leg upright before the glue sets. You can cure persistent leaning by propping up the leg with a length of scrap wood while the glue sets.

If the leg has split around the joint area, remove it, and clean the joint faces. Clamp the leg in a vice (vise), so that you can get at the splits easily. You have to get as much glue as possible deep inside the cracks, and then force the damaged parts together until they set. Animal glue cools and thickens too quickly to be of use here, but ordinary PVA (yellow) woodworking glue, thinned with 25 per cent volume of water, will usually do the job. Force the split apart with a chisel or screwdriver and push as much glue as you can into the joint with a paintbrush. Then bind the crack up tightly with rubber strips or hold it shut with screw clamps. Wipe away any surplus glue while it is still wet, or remove it with methylated spirits (wood alcohol).

The simplest way to repair a broken tenon on the end of the frame is to cut the damaged stub of the tenon off, make a new one and let it into a notch in the end of the frame. Use well-seasoned old wood for this job, and measure and mark the shape of the replacement tenon carefully. Cut the joint faces with a saw, and pare them to fit with a sharp chisel. When the part repairs are complete, reassemble the frame, making sure that the whole assembly is not twisted out of shape.

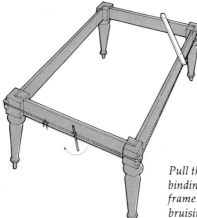

Pull the joints tight with a rope binding twisted round the whole frame. Protect the legs against bruising with scraps of carpet.

Fitting a false tenon

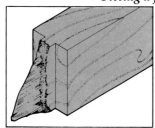

1 Cut a slot in the rail as thick as the broken tenon.

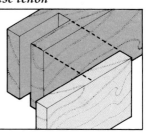

2 Make the false tenon twice the length of the original.

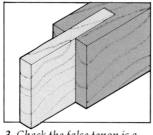

3 Check the false tenon is a snug fit then glue it.

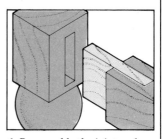

4 Reassemble the joint and clamp the table tightly.

Drawer repairs

Most traditional kitchen tables were fitted with drawers to hold the cook's tools and, since many of these were heavy, the drawer or the runners that support it eventually break. If the parts have not been lost, it is relatively easy to glue them back in place, but, if too much is missing, you will have to make a complete drawer.

Making traditional drawers

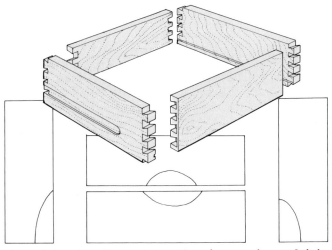

An exploded view of the parts to cut to make a new drawer. Label each before you start, to avoid confusion later.

Your drawer will look better if you can use old wood, and if you have an old chest drawer that can be altered to fit your table, it will save you some work. If you must make the drawer from new timber, use 22mm (⅞in.) thick for the front, of a type to match the rest of the table frame. Cut the sides and back from 10mm (⅜in.) boards and the bottom from 6mm (¼in.); this may be hard to find ready-made, so ask the lumber yard to prepare it. The sides, back, and bottom can be made from oak or high-grade joinery pine. Cut the drawer front, which should be a very tight fit in the frame, first. Make the sides the same width as the front and work out their length from the old runners, which will show signs of wear along the length of the original drawer. Cut the back exactly the same length as the front and around 20mm (¾in.) narrower.

Cutting the joints

The traditional joint used in drawer parts is the dovetail, for which you will need a marking gauge, a fine handsaw, and two chisels, one 6mm (¼in.), the other 10mm (⅜in.). To avoid confusion at the joint-cutting stage, mark each piece of wood before you begin. Set the gauge point to around 12mm (½in.) and, working from the inside face of the drawer front, scribe a line along each end of the drawer front. This line marks the 'lap', or amount that the drawer sides are let into the front. Without altering the gauge, scribe a line all round the front end of the sides. Now set the gauge to the exact thickness of the drawer sides and mark a line all round the back end of each drawer side, and round both ends of the drawer back. Set out the dovetails as illustrated below. When you have a complete set of parts, glue them together. The drawer bottom should be inserted into a groove, and note that the grain runs from side to side. Finally, plane the drawer sides until the drawer runs smoothly in and out.

Making a dovetail joint

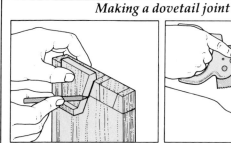

1 Mark the dovetail on the drawer side down to the lap.

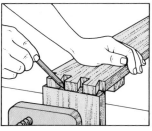

2 Saw carefully down the lines with a fine dovetail saw.

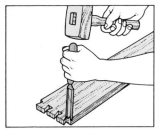

3 Chisel out the sockets with a sharp chisel and mallet.

4 Use the side as a template for the back and front.

Project 3: Blanket chest

Types of chest

Wooden chests and boxes have always been popular items of furniture, made by generation after generation of craftsmen, who either followed the fashion of the day, or imitated the taste of their forebears. There was a strong tradition in mainland Europe of giving a bride her trousseau in a stout chest, and in many poor homes such an item was the main piece of furniture, serving as table, wardrobe, linen store and seat. Many were taken to America by European immigrants, and a large number were built in the United States by the early settlers. Also found in the US are the smaller and usually more highly decorated Bible boxes. These share many features with their bigger cousins, and can be regarded as the same for restoration purposes.

The most common kinds of chest are the framed – the best, since its more complicated construction resists damp or very dry conditions better – and the 'country', which is made from plain wide boards, nailed up to form a box, and is less resistant to damage of all kinds. Inside both types there may be drawers, or a fixed inner tray with a lift-up lid. These chests were usually lined although the original lining may be missing.

Diagnosing faults

The parts of a chest most vulnerable to damage are the base and the lid. The base may be a simple skirting, sometimes called a plinth, or, less commonly, the chest may sit on four turned feet. Another alternative is that the end boards of a solid chest may sweep down below the box bottom and have been cut to form two legs at each end. This type of foot is a sign of an early piece. The most common problems with bases are that any decorative moulding may have been lost and will have to be replaced, and that the blocks which strengthen the skirting may have become loose.

The lids of almost all chests are made from solid boards, fixed together to form a single piece. The excessive dry heat of central heating causes the boards to twist or split and this, along with breaks around the lock or hinges, is the most common form of lid damage.

Left: *This framed blanket box* (top) *with its carved and moulded skirting is based on a traditional design. Once renovated, these boxes can enhance any room.*

Removing linings

In simple chests, you may find a decorated paper lining, often on top of a layer of newspaper, which can give some idea of when the piece was manufactured. Panelled boxes were usually lined with cloth pinned on to the inside. If the lining is in poor condition, or you are going to be doing major work on the box, you will have to remove it. The best way to do this with paper linings is to soak them off, rather as if you were stripping wallpaper. Cloth linings were generally pinned in place, but may also have been glued around the edges.

If the linings are original, you should keep them and re-attach them when you have finished all the structural work. In this case, it is essential to take great care when you are removing them. Old fabric can be strengthened before replacement by bonding fine calico (muslin) to the back. Heat beeswax in a waterbath as described for animal (scotch) glue on pp. 22-3, and brush a thin film on to the calico, then press the old fabric on to the waxy surface with a warm iron.

The best way to strengthen paper linings is to attach them to well-washed cotton sheeting with a thin coating of ordinary wallpaper paste.

Base repairs

If the base of your chest is of the simple skirting type, you should clean any old glue off the surfaces with water and a scraper and then simply reglue the loose parts in place.

Missing parts are more difficult to deal with because although the overall shape may be easy to make, there will probably be moulded or carved detail on the edges or front face. Short lengths of moulding are best made with a scratch-stock, which is discussed on p. 9. In order to use this to make a custom moulding, you will need to file a small piece of sheet steel to the right shape. The best way to do this is to keep filing away at the steel, fitting it to the shape of the remaining moulding as you work. When this cutter is the right shape, mount it in the stock.

Clamp the replacement piece of skirting in the vice (vise), grasp the scratch-stock firmly in both hands, and push it along the edge of the board. Press the side of the stock against the face of the board, keeping the moulding straight; the horizontal leg will limit its depth. The

Making a replacement moulding

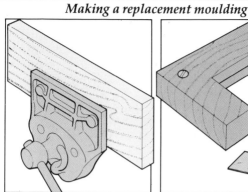

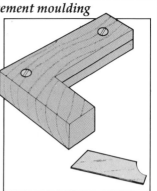

1 *Clamp the wood in the vice with the top square.*

2 *Fit the steel cutter into the scratch-stock.*

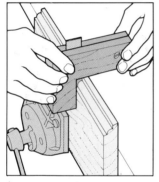

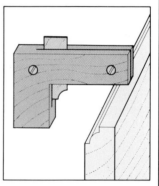

3 *Push the scratch-stock along the edge of the wood.*

4 *The finished profile should fit the cutter exactly.*

steel cutter will gradually scrape away the surplus timber until the moulding is the finished shape. When this is done, trim and mitre the new piece of skirting, then glue it in place.

Skirtings are often strengthened behind with rows of small wooden blocks glued into place with animal glue. These often work loose and are lost, so if you need to replace them, cut lengths of wood about 50-100mm (2-4in.) long. Turn the chest upside-down, then coat the blocks with hot animal glue and press them firmly into place. Remember that with animal glue you must work quickly. A slight rubbing motion will help to squeeze out any excess glue, and make the block firm without any need for clamps or pins (nails).

Lid repairs

Box lids are often damaged by being opened too far, which strains the hinges, and sometimes pulls the screws out of the wood. As well as causing strain, and perhaps bending the hinges, this enlarges the screw holes and loosens the grip of the woodscrew threads. The best remedy is to take the hinges off completely, and carefully bend the leaves straight again. The enlarged holes in the lid can then be plugged with slivers of wood dipped in glue. These chests were fitted with many different types of hinges; the most common were tee hinges, made from iron, or more rarely, brass, but you might also find butt or leaf hinges, good-quality examples of which are made from cast brass. Although not common, wooden hinges are sometimes found on old chests, and are usually broken when found. In this type of hinge the only metal parts are the pins that run through the wooden hinge segments. The only good way to repair these is to let in new timber pieces and recarve the broken segments. With a little care this can be done in such a way that most of the new wood is concealed beneath the old surface.

Sometimes ordinary hinges damage the chest so much where they screw into it that you will have to glue in similar pieces of wood to mount the hinges on. Cut a suitable piece of old wood to the size and shape of the required insert, but leave it thicker than necessary. Place the shaped insert over the spot that it is to go in, and mark around it. With a saw and sharp chisel, chop out the cavity, shaving it smooth on the bottom, so that the insert beds down well. A wedge shape is best for these simple inserts since they will fit tightly when you

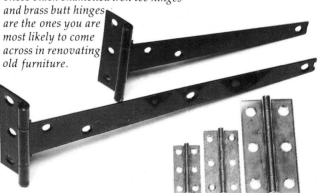

These black enamelled iron tee hinges and brass butt hinges are the ones you are most likely to come across in renovating old furniture.

push them into the gap. Spread a brushful of animal glue into the recess and insert the block immediately. Clamp it into position while the glue dries. After 24 hours, trim the block down flush with the surface using a sharp plane, set to take off a fine shaving, and refit the hinge. This is also a good way to repair damaged wood-work around locks.

Another common problem with chest lids is warping (curling) of the timber. There is no guaranteed cure for this problem, but it sometimes helps to veneer the convex side of the lid with some matching wood veneer. As this dries it will shrink and should pull the curl out of the top. More details on hinges are given on pp. 70-1 and on veneering on pp. 56-9.

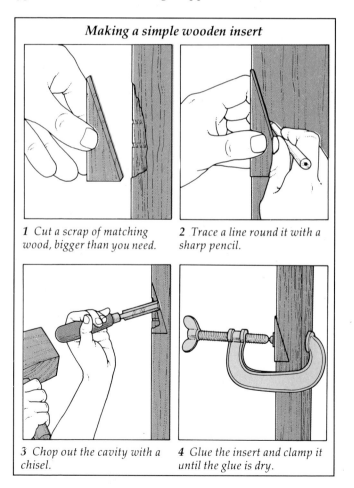

Making a simple wooden insert

1 Cut a scrap of matching wood, bigger than you need.

2 Trace a line round it with a sharp pencil.

3 Chop out the cavity with a chisel.

4 Glue the insert and clamp it until the glue is dry.

Project 4: Pine chest of drawers

Furniture for everyone

At the turn of the twentieth century, the great manufacturing centres of London and Philadelphia produced vast amounts of furniture, much of it solid and middle-class to suit the widening prosperity of the age. The increasing use of machinery concentrated production into ever bigger factories, and began to squeeze out the small workshops who had catered for this market. Many survived by producing for the city workers inexpensive versions of the mahogany and cherrywood pieces made for the better-off. The chest of drawers illustrated is a perfect example of this kind of furniture. Made from white pine, but polished (finished) to look like the more costly mahogany, the chest's sides and top are cut from single wide boards, and the sides are let into grooves beneath the top. Drawer supports are nailed straight on to the sides, and the front rails – the parts in between the drawers – are fixed in with mortise and tenon joints. The drawers themselves are dovetailed. Everything in the piece was done for simplicity and cheapness, but the overall effect is pleasing, and it has stood the test of time fairly well.

Diagnosing faults

A preliminary examination of the chest reveals that the back-boards are damaged, and all the drawer bottoms have shrunk, so that they have pulled out of the drawer-front grooves. The stops that prevent the drawers being pushed in too far are broken, or missing, and two of the drawer runners have broken away from their mountings. The surface, made of a softer wood than most furniture, is dented and cut here and there, and the polish has discoloured to a livid purply-red. As always, it is important for the restorer to decide in advance the order in which to tackle the problems. If the carcase (case) is badly damaged, that should be your first priority. Next, repair the drawers themselves, then tackle the rest of the carcase work. The surface can then be re-polished. Leaving this until last will give you a chance to blend in new parts or patches.

Left: *An incomplete attempt to strip this chest, and broken drawer runners and stops made it a sorry sight* (top). *Basic restoration and gentle stripping of the old polish have improved its appearance enormously.*

Repairing the back

Damaged or missing back-boards are common on old furniture, because the wood used for those parts that did not show, like the back and the dustboards fitted between each layer of drawers, was of the poorest quality. Backs usually consist of two or more boards, nailed on and fitted between strengthening uprights called muntins (stiles). These dividers, which stiffen large, thin panels, are also found in doors and on the bottoms of large drawers. Muntins may have grooves along each edge, or have a step-shaped reduction in the edge thickness, called a rebate or rabbet. Panels are either tapered to slip into the groove or, on cheaper work, are trapped under the edge of the rabbet when the muntins are fixed to the carcase.

The thin wood used for chest backs is easily damaged. If you can't cannibalize old work for replacements, try using the dustboards; they were often made from a similar wood.

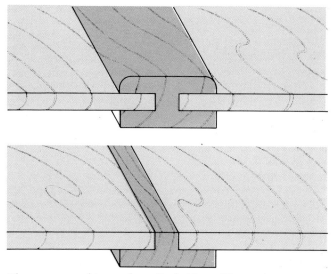

There are several types of muntin, but two of the most common are the grooved, which is usual in the bottoms of large drawers, and the rebated, more usual on cabinet backs.

The back panels and muntins of our chest are made from white pine. Better-class British pieces may have backs of oak, or, if they were made in the early twentieth century, of soft, greenish canary wood (poplar). Replacing the back panels will be difficult, unless you have access to old work that can be cannibalized for spare wood. The chief problem is that it is difficult to find wide, thin boards of any quality. There are two possible solutions you can adopt. The first is to replace the back-boards with plywood panels. Cut them to the same width as the old boards, then slip them between the muntins and nail them home.

The alternative is to look inside the chest for dustboards. These are protected from the hazards of moving house, and so on, and often survive intact. The dustboards are also, usually, cut from the same, or very similar, timber as the back panels. Remove the dustboards and recut them to make new back panels. Replace them with plywood panels, cut to size and fitted into the dustboard grooves inside the chest.

Remember that you should only adopt these solutions if you are certain that your piece is not a 'classic' (and, therefore, valuable) antique. Pieces of distinction should always be restored using completely authentic materials, or a considerable loss in value will result.

Repairing drawers

As long as all the parts are intact, most drawer repairs are fairly easy. Basic instructions on how to make replacement drawers are given on pp. 34-5. In furniture made before the twentieth century, drawer bottoms are usually of solid timber, rather than plywood. Since natural timber changes in size with varying humidity, there was always some movement of the drawer parts through the seasons. Central heating and air conditioning reduced this effect to a certain extent, but have brought a new problem. Modern homes are excessively dry, and since our antiques were built to live in a more natural environment, actual harm is caused by shrinkage of all the parts. Indeed, in some cases valuable pieces have been ruined almost beyond repair by modern hot, dry conditions.

Drawer bottoms

Drawer bottoms tend to shrink in width, that is, at right angles to the grain; timber shrinks only minutely along the grain lines. They are never glued, but slide into grooves at the front and sides of the drawer and, with time, they are pulled out of the groove at the front. This means that the drawer bottoms are unsupported and prone to damage during use. To repair this fault, remove the nails or screws holding the bottom to the back of the drawer, and push the drawer bottom firmly back into its slot – there is usually enough spare timber at the back of the drawer to do this – and then replace the fastenings along the back.

Shrinkage often causes drawer bottoms to pull out of the groove on the drawer front.

Drawer runner repairs

With the passage of time, the constant opening and closing of drawers results in the wooden runners which support the drawers becoming deeply grooved. This often causes the drawer fronts to sag out of line with the front of the piece. Similarly, the drawer sides also tend to wear along the rubbing surfaces. The best way to cure this is to level the affected parts with a plane, and once the surface is flat, to build it up to the right height with a slip of wood.

While the work is in progress, check constantly that you are keeping the surface flat. The edge of a steel rule is an ideal guide for this.

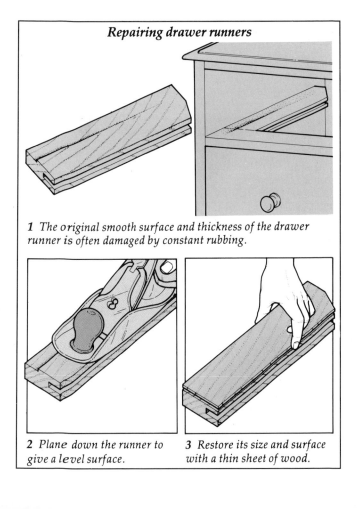

Repairing drawer runners

1 The original smooth surface and thickness of the drawer runner is often damaged by constant rubbing.

2 Plane down the runner to give a level surface.

3 Restore its size and surface with a thin sheet of wood.

Carcase repairs

When the drawers are running smoothly again and all the major structural problems have been attended to, minor repairs to the body of the chest, or carcase, can begin. Most old chests tend to lose the small wooden drawer stops, which are glued and pinned to the front rails and prevent the drawer from being pushed right back into the chest. You can make replacements from scraps of wood about 4-6mm (³⁄₁₆-¼in.) thick, shaped as shown below. When you are replacing them, take care to set the stops in the right position, so that the drawers line up well when they are closed.

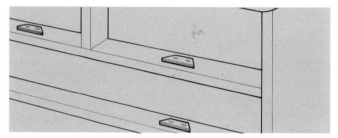

Take care when you position replacement drawer stops that the distance from the front of the chest to the stop is exactly the same as the width of the drawer front.

Repairing mouldings

Mouldings on chests are usually found around the top, around the base, or around or on the drawer fronts. There are two kinds of top and base moulds, worked mouldings – which are made on the edges of a large solid piece – and stuck mouldings, which as their name suggests are made separately and then stuck on. Mouldings on or around the drawer fronts are generally stuck. All these can be of almost any shape, though some types were associated with particular periods. You should look closely to see whether the mouldings are cut from cross-grained wood or not. Cross-grain walnut was used principally on high-class furniture of the late-seventeenth century, and you should treat any piece bearing this type of moulding as being of high potential value. The usual problem with cross-grain moulds is cracking or looseness, which you can fix by carefully gluing the mould in place, and filling the cracks with slips of matching timber.

The simplest method of repair for ordinary moulds of all kinds is to cut away any badly damaged portion and insert a block of new wood. Glue and clamp the block into place, and when it has set firm, roughly trim it to shape with a small plane. The final work of shaping and smoothing can be done with carving tools or the scratch-stock (see p. 9). Where mouldings are missing or badly damaged, it is best to replace the whole lot with a length of ready-made moulding from a cabinet-making or picture-framing specialist. The tiny half-round mouldings, called cock-beads, used around drawers are hard to make, and should also be bought.

Finally, you might be lucky enough to find old-style wooden moulding planes, which will help you to make a really authentic repair.

A simple moulding (top) *can be shaped in position with planes and sandpaper. More complex moulds* (bottom) *are best made with the scratch-stock.*

Blending old and new

When all the structural repairs are done, and everything is running smoothly again, you should make good any surface defects. Bear in mind that the sheen or patina of old furniture is built up over many years of wear and, if you have had to strip a surface, or fill in cracks in a large piece like a chest of drawers, you cannot hope to achieve this appearance of age and loving care immediately. Be patient, and let time, exposure to light, and regular dusting finish what you have started.

Trade techniques

Contrary to what many people think, wood polishers (finishers) do not achieve their results with wood dyes and polish alone. In fact, this is seldom the case, and most craftsmen use pigment as well as dye in order to match parts. A list of the most useful restorers' polishing materials is given on pp. 10-11. Many of these are difficult to obtain, and you will probably have to look through craft magazines for sources of supply.

Colour matching

Wood colours are based on combinations of red and black, with the addition of yellow, and sometimes green. By using dyes of these basic colours, perhaps with the addition of paint pigment, you can match any surface shade, although it will take time, so be patient. Try to work in good natural light only, and begin with a mix that is lighter than you need and darken it gradually until it matches. Water stains, based on cloth dyes, are very good for a foundation colour. Follow this with spirit (alcohol-soluble) colours, and when that layer is dry, overpaint it with pigments, or artist's water colours to achieve the correct appearance. An advantage of using this progressive system is that, if you make a mistake, you can remove the last layer without disturbing the one beneath. Use the appropriate solvent to remove any layer which is not right. Lines to imitate the grain of wood surrounding a patch can be added with water colour and a fine brush. After your surface repairs, seal the wood with a coat of french polish, diluted with an equal volume of methylated spirits (wood alcohol). Use a soft cotton pad and apply the solution as quickly as you can.

Repairing a damaged surface

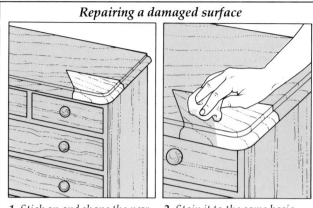

1 Stick on and shape the new wood.

2 Stain it to the same basic colour, and seal.

3 Paint in grain lines with water colours.

4 Seal the surface with a coat of french polish.

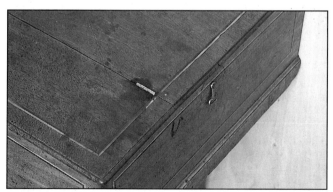

The surface of this piece has many marks, but patination like this adds charm.

Project 5: Regency side table

British classic style

The British Regency is considered to be the last clearly identifiable period of classic craftsmanship and the light and elegant furniture developed from the designs of Thomas Sheraton inspired many copies. Regency furniture was usually veneered, often in exotic woods like rosewood and zebrano; and leather-lined desk and table tops with gilt border tooling also appeared. Surface decoration of this kind of furniture was minimal, except for brass or wood inlaid lines, called 'stringing', and contrasting borders of wood veneer. The surfaces were mainly flat, with the exception of turned table or chair legs, and the pieces depended on refinement of shape for their effect.

Examining for defects

Although often exceptionally well-made, much of this kind of furniture is fragile, and veneered surfaces and sabre legs are both inherently prone to damage. The sabre leg, a typical Regency feature, has a built-in weakness. Its curved shape means that some weak, short, grain is included in the leg, and this makes them liable to snap. Even after 1810, when the design of these tables started to change and the legs were clustered around a central support, the basic sabre curve with its faults was retained. In this type of table support, there is the additional problem that the legs tend to splay out, snapping their joint to the central supporting piece. This is a tricky repair job, but can be successful if you tackle each stage with great care.

Veneers may be lost or damaged and also suffer from the effects of dry air, which shrinks the veneers and their groundwork differently, causing them to separate. Drop-leaf tables suffer from this problem too, since reduction in the size of the top gives too little room for the leaves to lower, and causes them to be prised away from their hinges.

The first thing to do is to examine the damage closely, to determine the correct method of working. With veneered pieces, tackle the structural work first, leaving the surfaces until last.

Left: *This reproduction Regency sofa table* (top) *has the classic double column and sabre leg. The nineteenth-century table* (bottom) *is halfway between sofa and dining table.*

Making a new leg

If the only problem with your table is loose joints, follow the advice given on pp. 20-1. If there was a lot of short grain included in the table leg, and it has snapped, you will have to make a new leg. This can be difficult, since you have to preserve the shape of the leg, which generally tapers in two directions, and make the new part slightly thinner than the old, to allow for the thickness of the veneer used to match the old surfaces. Mark the curve of a sound leg on to a piece of plywood, and cut the shape out. Then, use this as a template and cut a replacement leg from a piece of sound mahogany or beech.

Attaching a new leg

The other structural problem you might find with a piece like this is in fixing a new leg into the table's joint – a tapered dovetail housing, which is found in table pillars right up to the early twentieth century. Once the table has been assembled and glued, the leg cannot be removed from the joint without breaking it. This break occurs either by tearing timber from the support, which widens the housing enough for the leg to pull out, or by stripping wood away from the tongue on the end of the leg, with the same result. Of the two, the latter is easiest to deal with, since you will have less trouble camouflaging the repair.

The classic sabre leg: problems occur because the curved shape means that there is inevitably some short grain included

Cutting a new tongue

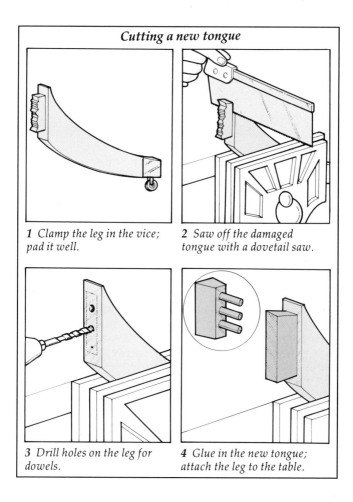

1 *Clamp the leg in the vice; pad it well.*

2 *Saw off the damaged tongue with a dovetail saw.*

3 *Drill holes on the leg for dowels.*

4 *Glue in the new tongue; attach the leg to the table.*

The damaged support can be dealt with by cutting the material away on each side of the joint. Cut new cheeks and glue them into position, taking great care to make them of the right thickness. When the glue has set, carve and sand the new cheeks to match the outside shape of the support. Clean the leg and apply fresh glue, then tap it back into place with a mallet.

If wood has been stripped from the tongue on the end of the leg, cut off the old tongue, leaving the surface of the leg flush, then cut a new tongue. Test its fit inside the housing, and when you are satisfied that it is a snug, but not tight, fit, fix it to the leg with dowels (see pp. 12-13). When the glued dowels have dried, apply glue to the joint faces, and reassemble the support.

Veneer repairs

Veneering is the art of covering surfaces with thin sheets of decorative material, in the cabinet-maker's case, wood. There were many reasons for using this technique on furniture, and it should not be seen merely as a way for makers to deceive their clients. Many of the timbers used for veneering old furniture were too weak, unstable, or rare to be used for construction, so pieces were made from sound, but plain, timber and then beautified with good-looking, but possibly capricious, materials. As the years go by, however, the glue used to unite the two layers loses its power to hold them. The result is a loosening of the surface skin, giving rise to bubbles, holes, and large-scale peeling.

Repairing blisters

Blisters, small patches of veneer which have lifted away from the surface, can usually be made to lie down again with a little heat and pressure. Take a steel cabinet scraper, and drop it into boiling water. Leave it until it is thoroughly heated, and then clamp it down firmly over the blistered patch. It is best to put a sheet or two of thick blotting paper between the metal and the wood, and a couple more over the steel to keep the heat in. Once again speed is essential, so that the hot steel remelts the glue beneath the blister, and allows it to re-adhere. This method has the advantage that it does not remove the surface polish. Any marking of the surface can be removed with 0000 grade steel wool.

This bureau has been extensively reveneered; here, the new veneer has been laid very wet, so that it will shrink (and age) quickly.

Patching veneer

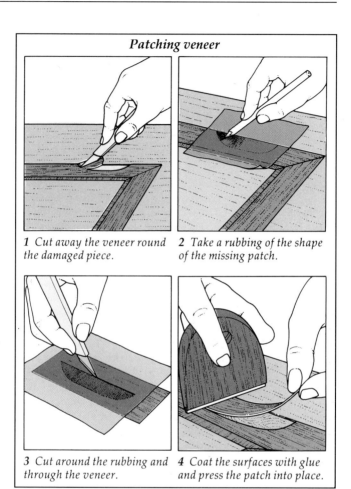

1 Cut away the veneer round the damaged piece.

2 Take a rubbing of the shape of the missing patch.

3 Cut around the rubbing and through the veneer.

4 Coat the surfaces with glue and press the patch into place.

Missing veneers

Lost veneers can be replaced fairly easily; the most difficult task is to find a good matching piece to insert. Old veneers are very thick, and it is almost impossible to obtain this saw-cut veneer today. Specialist veneer merchants advertise in the craft press, and you will probably have to take what they can offer. You may need two or more layers of modern thin veneer to build the surface up to the right level.

Take care when you cut out a patch to match the markings on the surface as far as possible; this will make your repair fit in better with the original. Stick the patch as described above.

Veneering large areas

Where veneers have become detached from the ground that supports them over a large area, the only sure way of refixing them is to remove, reglue, and press them down again. This will damage a polished surface, so you will have to repolish when the repair is complete.

Removing old veneers

You can exploit the reversibility of animal (scotch) glue when you want to remove old veneers. You will need a household iron, wet cloths, a thin-bladed knife, and a wallpaper scraper; these should do most of the work. Start by removing the polish, as this prevents moisture penetrating the surface. Shellac polish can be removed with methylated spirits (wood alcohol), but the varnishes more usual on American furniture will need paint stripper (see pp. 28-9). When the polish has gone, heat up the iron, set for 'Cotton', wet the surface of the veneer, put a damp cloth between the iron and the veneer and apply the iron lightly. Start by an edge of the piece. After a moment, remove the iron, and with the knife-blade, carefully prise (pry) up the veneer from the ground. If you have created enough hot steam, the veneer should peel away from its support easily. Once you have a fair-sized piece lifted, start using the wallpaper scraper. Work steadily along the piece, melting the old glue with the iron as you go. This is quite an easy trick to learn, and even large panels can be stripped quickly.

Laying veneer

Whether you are laying new veneer panels, or re-laying an old surface, the method is the same. Clean old veneer carefully with warm water, and do the same for the groundwork. New veneer need not be washed, but both old and new must be perfectly flat before you start laying so interleave them with cheap white paper, and press them for 48 hours, as if you were flower-pressing. Clamps on the outside of the boards will increase the pressure. When you lay the veneer, start at the centre, and heat the dampened veneer with the iron, so that the glue melts. Push any excess glue out with the veneer hammer. Try not to overheat the panel, as this will burn the glue and destroy its power of adhesion.

Re-laying a sheet of veneer

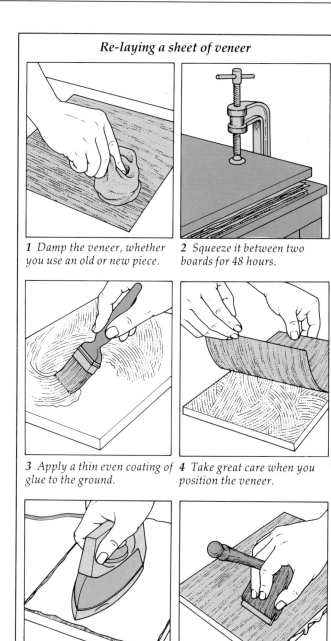

1 Damp the veneer, whether you use an old or new piece.

2 Squeeze it between two boards for 48 hours.

3 Apply a thin even coating of glue to the ground.

4 Take great care when you position the veneer.

5 Heat the veneer with the iron to remelt the glue.

6 Push out any excess glue with the veneer hammer.

Project 6: Sabre leg chair

Egypt and Trafalgar

Thomas Hope, a notable influence on art and architecture, is credited with the introduction in Britain of flat-sided chairs, which are based on illustrations in ancient Egyptian records. The interest in classical arts was such that the design soon became very fashionable, and many variations on the basic structure were produced. The version illustrated opposite is an early Victorian chair. Its simple appearance conceals precise and complicated internal joints. Brass lines and inlay patterns are also common on chairs of this type, originally made to celebrate Nelson's victory at Trafalgar.

The structure of these chairs was radically different from anything that had gone before, and reflects the enthusiasm for bold and uncluttered lines so typical of the Regency. The apparently simple construction is not without its drawbacks, however. The sweeping curves of the sabre legs mean that almost inevitably some of the parts were cut from wood with the grain lines running across, rather than along them. This makes these parts liable to break under pressure. The rope mouldings, also, are fragile and cane seats, common on this type of chair, are also prone to damage – they usually sag or split. Caning seats is really outside the scope of this book, indeed many professional restorers have this work done by people who are themselves experts. We will, however, consider the most usual types of fracture, and how to treat them, and also explain how to carve a replacement for the curved back rail.

Before you begin any major repair work, try to determine what wood the chair is made from. Mahogany, walnut and rosewood were the most common materials used for these chairs, although cheaper types were sometimes made in beech. The rarer American variants may be in cherry or maple. Recognizing the type of timber used is often difficult but as a general guide, mahogany of this period will be dark reddish-brown, with tiny white flecks in the cut surface. Walnut is pale golden-brown, and often strongly patterned; rosewood is heavy, oily, and a rich purplish-brown; cherry is faintly marked, and a warm mid-brown; both beech and maple are paler creamy woods. If your chair is maple, it is probably American.

Left: *This Victorian version of the flush-sided chair has sturdier front legs, but the weak back has damaged the seat frame* (inset).

Front leg repairs

As we have seen, classic flush-sided chairs have some weaknesses 'built-in', as a result of their design. Later examples of flush-sided chairs have turned front legs like the one illustrated. These are usually stronger than sabre legs, since they are made from straight-grained timber. Breaks in turned legs usually occur just below the joint (the joint at the top of the leg rarely breaks).

Turned leg repairs

Chair legs must be dowelled together wherever possible, for strength and safety. The most difficult part of the job is aligning drilled holes for a dowel to fit into. The best way round this problem is to drill deep into the broken-off part of the leg, then saw neatly through the leg at a convenient point near the break. Glue the sawn-off section back on to the chair, and, when the glue has set, use it to guide the drill into the chair frame. When a dowel is glued into place, it will strengthen and align all three pieces perfectly.

Knee joints

Earlier chairs, with sabre legs front and back, also have a more fragile joint between the leg and seat frame, often called the knee joint. Knee joints are tricky items to deal with. A tidy repair can often be made merely by gluing the parts together again, but this will leave the chair dangerously weak. In severe cases, the only remedy is to make a new upper leg and knee.

Most knee joints are variations on the mortise and tenon. The tenon is usually undamaged, but you should clean off the old glue, then use the damaged part of the leg as a pattern to make a new section. Graft this on to the old leg as described on pp. 64-5. Cut the mortise holes after you have joined the old and new sections; take the sizes and angles of the joint parts from the old pieces. Work slowly – this is a skilled job.

Mark out with a gauge, or sharp knife, to give a thin clear line. Chop the mortises with a strong narrow chisel. Start in the middle, and work towards the ends, squaring the hole up as you go – drilling out the waste saves time and effort. Glue on and clamp the complete leg, carefully aligning it with its companion.

Repairing a turned leg

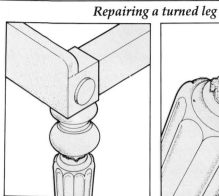

1 Breaks in turned legs usually occur near the joint.

2 Drill deeply into the broken-off part of the leg.

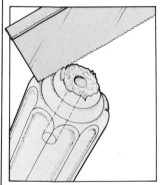

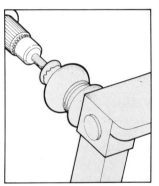

3 Saw across the broken piece below the break.

4 Glue to the frame; use as a guide for drilling.

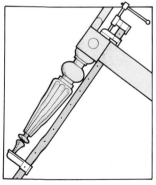

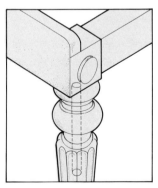

5 Clamp the pieces together while the glue dries.

6 A dowel holds all three pieces together.

Broken backs

The sweeping sabre curves of this type of chair may lead to problems with the rear frame members. The most usual fault is splitting or failure of the lower section of the legs, often caused, like so many problems with chairs, by them being dragged across carpets or tipped back while someone is seated. The break is generally a long one when it occurs here and can often be rejoined with glue. As always, clean the surfaces carefully before you start gluing. Rubber lashings will hold the parts still while the glue is setting.

Since the results of a sudden failure of a repair of this type can be dangerous for sitter and seat alike, many restorers like to reinforce the glued joint with dowels or pegs. This is best done after the two parts have been joined. One very good method is to use slim dowels made from split cane. The thin pieces of bamboo sold for garden use will provide hundreds of very strong dowels at low cost. These should be inserted at an angle to increase the strength of the joint – the downward force will tend to push the two parts more closely together. More complex breaks in the back frame may have to be dealt with by inserting a new section, in the same way as described for knees on p. 62.

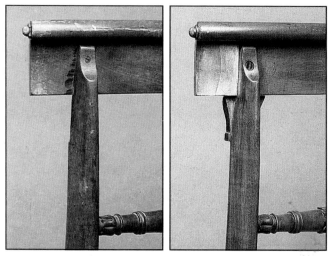

A loose joint between the crest rail and the back upright has resulted in wood flaking away round the joint. The repair involves cutting a smooth wedge-shaped slice away from the damaged portion, then gluing in and carving an insert to shape.

Sabre leg repairs

1 Trace the shape of a good leg on to the timber.

2 Cut damaged stub to give a clean surface.

3 Trim new part and fix to broken leg.

4 Glue, dowel and sand new part to shape.

Broken back rails

The curved cross rails on the upper back of typical flush-sided chairs are a challenge for the restorer. Often they are so badly damaged that complete new parts must be made. If repair seems possible, then follow the methods described on pp. 48-9 and 68-9. If you need to make a new part, put a large square of wood off-centre in the lathe and, turning it very slowly, work the pins that fix the rail in the chair frame, and the small bobbin ornaments at each end. Techniques for turning are given on pp. 20-1. When these are done, mark the curved shape of the rail between the turned portions, and cut away the waste with a bandsaw or coping saw. Then, roughly shape the curved part with a rasp, or carving tools. If there is carved detail, you will have to add it by hand, after rough shaping. Many workers find it convenient to hold work of this kind in the lathe, where it can be rotated by hand, giving easy access to all sides.

Project 7: Pennsylvania Dutch dresser

The Germans of America

The first German colonists arrived in Pennsylvania in 1683, soon after the founding of the colony. These early settlers were relatively wealthy people, who brought with them their own belongings from the Rhinelands. The poorer 'Redemptioners' who came later were bonded labourers, and created their own homes with a grant of land and tools, given after they had discharged their obligations. These were all people who concentrated primarily on their homes and farms, and many of them became prosperous. The craftsmen developed a typical style of furniture, based on native German work, which was distinguished by elaborate painting and graining of the wood, and the use of intricate fret-cut scrolls. This type of furniture is usually called Pennsylvania Dutch, a corruption of *Deutsch*.

While eighteenth-century furniture of this kind is rare and expensive, good later examples are sometimes found, and the general principles of construction and restoration of this type of work apply to country furniture of all types.

Diagnosing problems

Made for everyday use in simple homes, most country furniture was extremely sturdy. The common failings are the results of ordinary wear and tear, and the excessive shrinkage caused by air-conditioning and central heating.

This type of furniture was often decorated with fretwork or scrollwork. Much of this was delicate and, naturally, in time pieces are broken off and some are lost completely. We will look at the ways to replace this work. Door damage is also very common on dressers. In some cases, the doors themselves split or crack, and sometimes the hinges break. Fixing hinges is not difficult, and we will examine the techniques involved. Finally, because this type of furniture was made for everyday use, surfaces often deteriorate, so we will consider ways of reviving finishes.

Left: *This handsome Pennsylvania Dutch dresser is now a valuable museum piece. Note the many small dents and scratches which the restorer aims to reproduce when 'distressing'. Simpler country pieces (inset) are still to be found at bargain prices. In this piece the doors have sagged a little, due to worn hinges.*

Repairing fretwork

There are two basic types of fretwork decoration on country furniture. The first, and most common, is properly called scrollwork, and consists of boards of 6mm (¼in.) thickness or more, scalloped on the edges and sometimes pierced through with decorated shapes. This type of work is found mainly on the tops and bases of all kinds of cabinet work, in varying degrees of complexity. Since it was often done in thin timber to reduce the labour of cutting, pieces tend to break off, and if the piece is old, inevitably some are lost. The best way to deal with this is to graft a new section on to the damaged frieze, and re-create its original form. If all of the shaped part is missing, you will have to look for similar pieces, and use patterns drawn from them to make a completely new replacement. Careful research will give a piece that will look harmonious with the whole and pass unnoticed by all but experts. The best way to graft a new piece on is to prepare a board of similar timber to the correct thickness, but allow extra on the length and width. The amount of this allowance will depend on the shape of the part to be replaced. Remove the old frieze, clamp the new board firmly behind the damaged part, and cut away the broken edge of the old part. It will not matter if the line is straight since the saw will also pierce the new board. This double-cut method will ensure a good fit when the new part is glued to the old. When the glue has set, mark the shape on to the new part, and cut it with a coping saw, an electric jigsaw or, if you are a real traditionalist, a bow-saw.

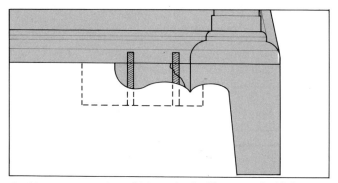

Grafting on a new piece of frieze: the double-cut method helps to ensure a good fit.

Ornamental fretwork

You may find thin plywood or solid timber fretwork, usually about 3mm (⅛in.) thick, stuck or pinned over a solid surface, or in dainty pieces, left unsupported and used to form gallery rails, decorative shelf edging or corner brackets. Cut new parts from thin plywood, which you can make from layers of decorative veneers.

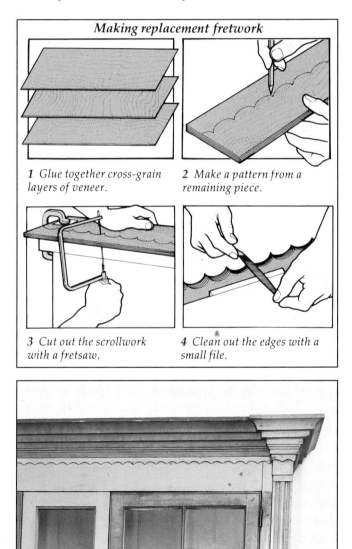

Making replacement fretwork

1 Glue together cross-grain layers of veneer.

2 Make a pattern from a remaining piece.

3 Cut out the scrollwork with a fretsaw.

4 Clean out the edges with a small file.

This cornice has applied fretwork, made from thin wood.

Fixing broken turnings

On pp. 20-1, we considered ways of making new turned parts. The repair of turnings is possible without the use of a lathe, however, so long as you have the main parts. The most satisfactory method of repair is to dowel the broken pieces together, in the same way as described for turned chair legs on pp. 62-3. For extra strength, use metal dowel, which is easily cut from carpentry nails of different sizes.

Hinge repairs

Broken door hinges and hinge fastenings are found repeatedly on cabinet furniture of all types and periods. There are many varying patterns of hinge but two basic types are found most often on country furniture. The particular kind favoured by makers of Dutch furniture is the surface-mounted hinge, which is generally made from iron or, more rarely, brass. The two leaves, or flaps, are cut into ornamental shapes along the margin. Damage to hinges usually consists of a broken or missing leaf, or a badly worn pin, which makes the hinge slack. This slackness makes the door droop, and causes further damage to both door and cabinet. Anyone with access to a metalwork shop can turn a new pin, but you can make sound repairs without access to expensive machinery.

If the hinge is intact, you will have to remove one leaf. Brass leaves should be softened by heating with a blowtorch, and plunging into cold water before you attempt this. The pin will be fixed into one leaf, and it is the other, 'loose leaf', that you should remove. This can be done by opening the rolled part with a screwdriver blade, until the two hinge leaves come apart. The worn pin will now be exposed, and can be built up with wire and plumber's solder. Use brass wire for brass hinges, and soft iron florist's wire for iron. Clean the wire and the pin carefully with emery paper, and then wrap the wire around the pin in a tight spiral. When the spiral is complete, hold the piece in tongs, and use liquid flux and plumber's solder to both bond the wires together, and bond them to the pin inside. Set it aside to cool and then file it to shape. The hard wire will resist wear for a long time. When the pin has been reshaped, replace the other side of the hinge and tap the 'wrap' shut with a small hammer.

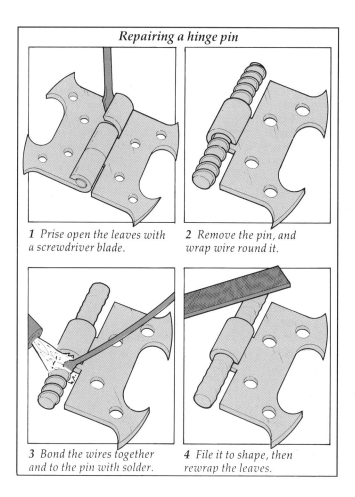

Repairing a hinge pin

1 Prise open the leaves with a screwdriver blade.

2 Remove the pin, and wrap wire round it.

3 Bond the wires together and to the pin with solder.

4 File it to shape, then rewrap the leaves.

Missing leaves are more difficult to fix, one of the problems being obtaining the right material to make the new part from. Old-fashioned ironbox locks, of the kind once used for house doors are a good source of soft iron sheet, and old brass may be found in the mechanisms of broken mantel-clocks of the 1950s. Make a pattern for the new leaf in card, and cut out the part with a small piercing saw. The wrap that goes round the pin can be partly formed by hammering around a nail, and finished in the same way as described for the pin repair opposite.

The more carefully engineered butt hinges are more difficult to repair, and you should look for a replacement, or seek help from an expert.

Door repairs

Broken hinges often lead to problems with doors. There are many potential sources of trouble here, but we will examine the most common. Breaks around the hinges are caused by excessive weight on the door. Small children are often at fault here, leaning heavily on the top of the door as they bend to peek inside. Where the hinge screws have simply pulled out, plug the holes with slivers of wood dipped in glue, and refix the hinges. Sometimes, the strain will break away a long strip of the wood. If the break is not too severe, simply reglue the wood, and strengthen it with small dowel rods (see pp. 12-13) after the glue has set. If the part is very badly broken, or missing, you must replace it.

The problem of finding timber to match the door can be overcome by cutting a square strip of material from the inside edge of the door with a tenon saw. Glue a piece of material, which need be only an indifferent match, into this rebate, and use the sawn strip as a source of exactly matching timber to replace the missing piece. This method can also be used to provide timber to build up the bottom of doors, where slack hinges have resulted in abnormal wear.

The only remedy for loose door joints, which cause the whole door to sag, is to dismantle the door, clean the joint surfaces, and reassemble it with fresh glue. Where the tenons are a loose fit into the corresponding mortise, spread them slightly with slim wedges let into saw-slots. Sometimes the secret wedged tenon (see pp. 12-13) will be a good method of stiffening joints, but try to avoid doing this, since modern restoration practice is not to do anything which could cause problems for future generations.

Replacing door panels

Sometimes, you will need to make a whole new door panel. Most doors on country furniture have simple fielded panels and, if you need to make one of these, a suitable piece of old furniture timber is almost essential, since new wood will rarely look 'at home'. Making fielded panels is a job where a spindle moulder or router comes in handy, although you can get good results by hand. Use a small shoulder plane to make the sloped fielding, and run it along a fence clamped to the work.

Repairing damage to doors

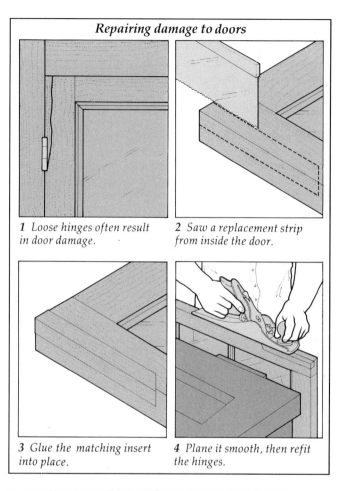

1 Loose hinges often result in door damage.

2 Saw a replacement strip from inside the door.

3 Glue the matching insert into place.

4 Plane it smooth, then refit the hinges.

This classic type of door has a fielded panel retained by a thin moulding, making it easy to remove.

Cleaning and reviving paint and polish

Painted and polished surfaces are often renewed quite unnecessarily, reducing the value of a piece in the process, since much of the patina that gives old things their beauty is lost. Careful cleaning can render refinishing totally pointless. Try the remedies here carefully and choose an unobtrusive spot to begin work, since the great variety of old finishes means that results can vary.

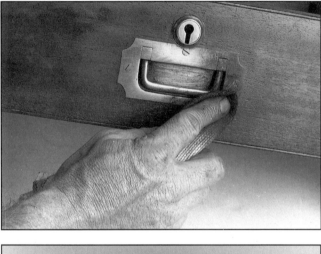

Metal fittings can usually be cleaned in position, but you should remove them for heavy cleaning. Final buffing of polished surfaces and metalwork demands soft, clean cloths – cotton are best.

Dirty paint

A gentle method for cleaning light grime is to dissolve 50g (2oz.) of common soda (baking soda) in 500ml (1 pint) of hot water. Dip a soft cloth in the mixture and squeeze it almost dry, then use it to wipe the surface over. Repeat this treatment with a cloth dipped in warm water with a little wine vinegar. Once again, keep the cloth almost dry. Leave the finish for two hours, then polish it with a soft, dry, cloth.

A more vigorous cleaner is made from equal parts of dishwashing liquid and white spirit (paint thinner). Shake well and set it aside until the mixture sets to a firm jelly, then rub it into the surface, and wipe it off with a clean damp cloth as you go. Do not leave it in contact too long, since it may soften some paints.

French polish

More common on British furniture, french polish looks like a thin glassy-smooth varnish. To make a reviver, mix 1 part shredded beeswax with 3 parts Mexican turpentine, 3 parts unboiled linseed oil, and 3 parts methylated spirits (wood alcohol). Stand this in a bowl of warm water, and shake it until the mixture is smooth. Apply it frugally with a soft polishing pad.

All-purpose cleaner

This mixture will remove old sticky wax and most other built-up dirt from all kinds of surface, and is particularly good for American varnish finishes. In a screw-top bottle mix one cupful of wine vinegar, one cupful of Mexican turpentine, one cup of boiled linseed oil, a quarter cup of methylated spirits, and a teaspoonful of strong ammonia. Apply with a soft paintbrush, and wipe off any excess with tissue or cloth.

Cleaning metal fittings

Commercial metal polishes are far too harsh to use routinely for cleaning old brass and iron fittings. By far the best material to use is jeweller's rouge. This is a fine red powder, and should be mixed for use with a little olive oil. Apply the paste with a pad, and remove it with a clean cloth. Severe corrosion can be removed with grade 0000 steel wool dipped in turpentine.

Acknowledgements

Swallow Books gratefully acknowledge the assistance given to them in the production of *Woodframe Furniture Restoration* by the following people and organizations. We apologize to anyone we may have omitted to mention.

Photographs: The American Museum in Britain 66, 69, 73; Jon Bouchier 1, 6, 8, 9, 11, 16, 18, 21, 22, 40, 42, 44, 46, 49, 51, 56, 60, 64, 74; Arthur Brett and Sons Ltd 52(T), 54; The Bridgeman Art Library 14, 52(B); Jaycee Furniture 36(T); Ronseal 4, 26(B), 28; Jessica Strang 26(T), 36.
(T) – Top; (B) – Bottom.

Tools on pages 8 and 9 supplied by E. Amette and Co Ltd.

Restoration: Sabre leg chairs, pages 60, 64 restored by Liz Dennes, London College of Furniture. Clock hood, page 49 restored by Peter Roose, London College of Furniture. Chest of drawers, pages 42, 44, 46, 49 restored by John Lonas, London College of Furniture.

Illustrations: Hussein Hussein 13, 30, 32, 33, 39, 45, 48, 63, 65, 68, 69, 71, 73; Aziz Khan 19, 21, 23, 25, 47, 55; Coral Mula 15, 29, 35, 41, 51, 57, 59; Rob Shone 12, 31, 34.

We are grateful to the London College of Furniture for their assistance in the preparation of this book.